# Great Pet Names

## By Dan Froseth

# Great Pet Names

## By Dan Froseth

## Published by

## Folsom, CA

ISBN #0-9637809-0-5

# Table of Contents

# Introduction

Your pet needs a name! And you're the lucky one that gets to choose it. What fun! But there are about a zillion possible names, and the one that is "just right" for your pet may not occur to you without a little help...

"Help" in this case is right in your hands in the form of hundreds of unique, fun, interesting, silly, distinguished names – all organized into neat, logical categories for easy reading.

You will find seven categories based on the basic characteristics your pet is likely to have now — or when it grows up. You probably know which category (or chapter) best fits your pet, so the search is already simplified! And your imagination may be triggered to come up with yet another neat name for your creature.

You may notice that almost all of the names in the various categories are only one or two syllables. This makes it easier for your pet to learn and recognize his or her name.

Choose a name that has a nice rhythm and ring to it (one that does not sound like any of the basic commands or the name of another household member). Does it fit? Does it sound and feel like your pet? If not, pick another. Your pet will be patient. They realize it takes time for us humans to be trained.

# Chapter One

# Comical Names

Comical, whimsical names for the pet that seems determined to go through life just for the fun of it — lots of laughs, lots of smiles, and lots of rollicking down "the sunny side of the street."

Abner
*Character from Al Capp's comic strip*

Ace

Adida

Airhead

Airmail

Alien

Alpo

Amazing

Amigo
*Spanish for "friend"*

Anchor

Angler

Ankle

Ark

Aspirin

Asset

Autumn

B.C.

Babble

Baboon

Babu

Bacon

Baffle

Bagle

Bail

Bailiff

Bait

Balk

Balky

Ballad

Baloney

Bard

Barefoot

Barfly

Bargain

Barkeep

Barracks

Barter

Baseball

Basket

Batman

Bayo

Bebop

Belt

Bessie

Bilge

Bimmer
*Nickname for a BMW*

Binder

Binge

Bingo

Bitchin

Blarney

Blather

Bleak

Bloke

Blowout

Bluegrass

Bo

Bogart

Bogey

Bomber

Bongo

Bonkers

Booboo

Boogie

Boomer

Boone

Bootleg

Boots

Bootsie

Bopper

Borg

Bouncer

Bounder

Bourbon

Boxcar

Bozo

Brandy

Breaker

Brig

Briny

Broadway

Broker

Bronco

Bronx

Brownie

Buckeye

Buckwheat

Budget

Buff

Bufus
*Slang for "beautiful"*

Bugle

Bumstead

Bungle

Burger

Bwana

Caboose

Cactus

Cajun

Cal

Calypso

Carefree

Carrot

Casino

Castro

Catcher

Catchup

Catfish

Chablis

Chaos

Cheddar

Cheers

Cheesecake

Chestnut

Chili

Chips

Chocolate

Chopper

Chow

Circus

Clerk

Clown

Clump

Coach

Coaster

Cockney
British for "a spoiled
child"

Coffee

Cool

Coot

Corky

Cowboy

Crackers

Crash

Crazy

Credit

Crocker
A "potter"

Curfew

Custer

Daffy

Dayo

Decoy

Digger

Dipper

Disco

Dixie

Dodge

Donut

Doodle

Doonesbury

Dork

Drummer

Drydock

Dude

Duster

Dweeb

Echo

Ego

Eightball

Elvis

Fantasy

Farce

Farout

Farside

Fastball

Fatcat

Fiddle

Fidel

Fizz

Flake

Flash

Flip

Flopsy

Football

Forgot

French

Friday

Frijole
*Spanish for "bean"*

Frisbee

Friskie

Frito

Fumble

Funky

Gabby

Gamble

Garfield

Georgia

Gizmo

Gogo

Goober
  *A peanut*

Goofy

Gringo
  *Spanish for*
  *"American"*
  *(derogitory)*

Grounder

Grumpy

Gypsy

Hack

Hagar

Ham

Happy

Harley

Harvord

Hawkeye

Heathcliff

Hershey

Hiccup

Hippie

Hobo

Hocky

Hokey

Hombre

Hoop

Hoosier
  *A native of Indiana*

Hooter

Horny

Hotdogger

Hunk

Iceberg

Igloo

Ignatz

Irish

J.R.

Jargan

Jarhead

Jazz

Jersey

Jethro

Jib
*A sailboat's sail
(nearest the bow)*

Jibe
*A sailing maneuver*

Jingles

Jock

Jojo

Joker

Jughead

Ketch

Ketchup

Kickoff

Kilroy

Kingfish

Kinky

Lampoon

Lark

Lawyer

Licker

Lightning

| | |
|---|---|
| Lingo | Mimic |
| Linus | *A great name for a parrot* |
| Logo | Mischief |
| Loto | Mogul |
| Lottery | Monday |
| Lotto | Monkey |
| Loulou | Monsoon |
| Lumni | Mopsy |
| Mach 1 | Moxy |
| Madonna | Muff |
| Magic | Muggs |
| Mallard | Mutt |
| March | Mystic |
| Mascot | Myth |
| MASH | NASA |
| Master | Nerd |
| Melon | Nike |
| Merchant | Noel |
| Midnight | Noodle |
| Miller | Nuke |

Nutmeg

Odie

Okie

Omen
*A sign of the future*

Oreo

Panchp

Patches

Paws

Pepper

Pepsi

Perky

Pogo

Pokey

Polo

Pongo

Poochkie

Pooper

Popcorn

Popeye

Popper

Porgy

Porky

Port

Prank

Primo

Putter

Quad

Quick

Rad

Radar

Ramble

Rascal

Reb

Rebel

Rebound

Refer

Reflex

Robot

Rockford

Rodeo

Rowdy

Ruff

Rum

Sagebrush

Sailor

Salty

Sambo

Sassy

Saucer

Sawdust

Scamp

Schnapps

Schooner

Scooter

Scotch

Scrappy

Scruggs

Secret

Sequel
*A continuation (last born?)*

Shadow

Shimmy

Shiner

Shoal

Shushu

Skeet

Sleeper

Slick

Slingshot

Slippers

Snackbar

Snafu
*Chaotic condition: Situation normal, all fouled up*

Snapper

Sneaker

Sniffles

Snipe

Snooker

Snoopy

Snorkel

Snowshoes

Soapbox

Soapy

Sober

Socks

Soda

Spanky

Sparkplug

Sparky

Splash

Spooky

Spooner

Stanford

Starboard
*Nautical term for right*

Stein

Stuffy

Sucker

Suds

Summer

Surf

Surfboard

Surfer

| | |
|---|---|
| Swinger | Treefrog |
| Tach<br>*Short for tachometer –<br>indicates RPMs* | Trek |
| | Trig |
| Taco | Tripod |
| Tailspin | *A pet missing one leg.<br>Booo!* |
| Take off | Trolley |
| Talker | Trump |
| Tangent | Tuesday |
| Tango | Tumbleweed |
| Tardy | Turnpike |
| Tater | Tutu |
| Tatters | Tux |
| Tattoo | Umpire |
| Tavern | Valium |
| Taxi | Vodka |
| Tic Tac | Wag |
| Tic Tock | Wahoo |
| Tinker | Whacker |
| Tippy | Whacko |
| Toad | Whiskey |
| Tramp | Winter |

| | |
|---|---|
| Wizard | Yogi |
| Wonk | Yogurt |
| Woofer | Yoyo |
| Yale | Zany |
| Yankee | Zero |
| Yodel | Zip |
| Yoga | Zsa Zsa |

# Chapter Two

# Affectionate Names

Affectionate names for the pet with a personality as sweet as honey and always in need of a hug or a pat on the head. (Please, no one-finger pats for Great Danes and no bear hugs for Toy Poodles.)

Ador

Angel

Azalea

Babe

Baby

Balmy

Bambi

Bashful

Beau
*Handsome or admirer*

Best

Biscuit

Blessed

Blueberry

Bonbon

Bonita
*Spanish for "pretty"*

Buddy

Buffie

Bunny

Buttercup

Butterfly

Buttons

Candy

Charm

Charming

Cherry

Chick

Chickie

Chum

Coquette
*A flirt*

Cotton

Crony

Cuddles

Cupcake

Cupid

Curly

Cutie

Cutsie

Dandy

Darling

Dawn

Dear

Dolce
*Italian for "sweet"*

Dove

Eros
*Greek god of love*

Faith

Fawn

Feather

Fifi

Flirt

Fluffer

Foxie

Frostie

Giggles

Ginger

Goddess

Grace

Honey

Hope

Iris

Jingle

Joy

Lady

Lilac

Lily

Lollipop

Lotus

Love

Lover

Manners

Mellow

Melody

Mercy

Miffy

Mimi

Model

Muffin

Music

Nice

Nugget

Nuzzles

Orchid

Panda

Pansy

Paramour
*A lover*

Passion

Patience

Peachie

Pearl

Perfect

Pet

Petunia

Poem

Poppy

Precious

Primrose

Puddin

Pumpkin

Punkie

Punkin

Pussy

Rainbow

Rose

Rosebud

Ruby

Saint

Satin

Sidekick

Silky

Smile

Smitten

Snuggles

Special

Spring

Squeaky

Squiggles

Style

Sugar

Sunny

Sunrise

Sunset

Sunshine

Sweetie

Super

Tadpole

Taffy

Tender

Tiffy

Tonic

Tootsie

Toy

Treasure

Treat

Trixie

Trophy

Tulip

Tumbles

Twinkie

Twinkles

Valentine

Velvet

Venus
*Roman goddess of love*

Whimpy

Wiggles

Winker

Zippy

# Chapter Three

# Aristocratic Names

The aristocratic category suggest names for the upper class members of the world of pets. These are characters not to be trifled with, who go trotting down life's pathways with four feet firmly on the ground and one haughty nose in the air. They may even insist that you address them as "Mister" or "Madam." And if they seem aloof and superior, they probably are.

Abbey

Actor

Admiral

Alexander

Allegro
*Musical term for quick and lively*

Alpha

Alto

Amanda

Anglo

Anthem

Apollo

Argus
*A watchful guardian*

Aristocratic

Aristotle

Armstrong

Arthur

Artist

Ascot

Ashley

Astro

Astroid

Athens

Atlantis

Azimuth

Bach

Bacon
*A philosopher*

Baden

Ballet

Bard
*A poet and singer of long ago*

Baron

Baroque

Basil

Bastille

Beethoven

Bentley

Berlioz

Bernard

Bernstein

Beta

Binary

| | |
|---|---|
| Bio | Cello |
| Bismark | Celt |
| Bizet | Cesanne |
| Bligh | Charles |
| Bonaparte | Chaucer |
| Bradford | Chic |
| Brahms | Chief |
| Brando | Chopin |
| Bravo | Classy |
| Bridgette | Cognac |
| Brutus | Colette |
| Caesar | Colonel |
| Camelot | Commander |
| Cameo | Commodore |
| Caprice | Conrad |
| *A sudden change of mind or whim* | Copland |
| Captain | Count |
| Cardinal | Credence |
| Carmen | Czar |
| Cathode | Dalton |
| Caviar | Dante |

Darwin

Deacon

Dean

Debate

Debussy

Delphi

Dewey

Doctor

Duchess

Duke

DuPont

Dvorak

Earl

Einstein

Entree

Epic

Epoch
*A period of time, an era*

Esquire

Falstaff

Frederick

Gandhi

Gatsby

General

Genghis

Gentry

Gershwin

Glory

Goethe

Grammar

Hamlet

Handel

Haydn

Hearst

Heather

Hector

Henry

Herod

Higgins

Hilton

Hobbs

Holmes

"Wanna chase a few?"

| | |
|---|---|
| Homer | Khan |
| Ingrid | *Title of respect in central Asia* |
| Irving | King |
| Jacques | LaSalle |
| Jessica | Laser |
| Joseph | Lear |
| Judge | Ledger |
| Julia | Levi |
| Jupiter | Lunar |
| Kaiser | Mahler |
| Kent | Major |

Malthus

Mandate

Marco

Marlowe

Marquette

Marshall

Mayor

McGraw

Melville

Melvin

Mentor
*Wise and trusted adviser*

Mercedes

Merger

Merit

Metric

Midas
*Greek legend of great wealth*

Misses

Mister

Mockup

Monarch

Monty

Morgan

Mozart

Napoleon

Neptune
*Greek god of the sea*

Nero

Newton

Noble

Nova
*An unusual star*

Oboe

Parson

Patron

Pavarotti

Pavlov

Pawn

Peace

Peerless
*Without equal, unmatched*

| | |
|---|---|
| Percy | Reason |
| Plato | Renee |
| Pluto | Rimsky |
| Poet | Ripley |
| Polar | Ritz |
| Prelude | Rolls |
| Presto | Roman |
| Prince | Rome |
| Princess | Romeo |
| Professor | Roxanne |
| Proton | Royal |
| Proverb | Rudyard |
| Puccini | Sabrina |
| Purcell | Samantha |
| Quantum | Saturn |
| *A major advance* | Schroeder |
| Queen | Schubert |
| Quota | Schumann |
| Quote | Seville |
| Rachael | Seymour |
| Randolph | Shah |
| Ravel | |

Shawn

Sheik

Sherlock

Shogun

Sibyl

Sigmund

Simon

Skipper

Solar

Squire

Stanza
*A group of lines in
poetry or music*

Sterling
*Genuine, reliable,
excellent*

Strauss

Tammy

Tanya

Thatcher

Thor

Tiffany

Tito

Topaz
*A gem*

Torry

Tort
*A law violation*

Travis

Treaty

Tribune

Truman

Tucker

Tutor

Twain

Tyler

Valiant

Vanessa

Vega

Venice

Verdi

Verdict

Vicar

Vicky

Virgil

| | |
|---|---|
| Wagner | Winston |
| Walter | Wizzard |
| Watson | Wolfgang |
| Wendy | Woodstock |
| Werner | Zenith |
| | *Highest point, apex* |
| Whitman | |
| | Zeno |
| Wilbur | |
| Windsor | |

"He wants you to notice his new ball."

# Chapter Four

# Big Names

If you expect (or fear) that your pet will become as huge as a hippo, choose a name from among these extra large labels.

Acre

Amazon

Ample

Angus

Atlas

Awesome

Ballast
*A heavy or stabilizing force*

Ballon

Barn

Barrell

Bass

Beam

Behemoth
*A large, powerful animal*

Big Al

Big Foot

Big Joke

Big Mac

Big Mo

Big Sur

Blimp

Boeing

Brawn

Brute

Bubba

Bulk

Bull

Burly

Caddie

Chubs

Cosmos

Cyclops
*Greek one-eyed giants*

Dallas

Empire

Giant

Glutton
*An over-eager eater*

Heavy

Heifer

Hippo

Horse

Hulk

Husky

Igor

Jumbo

Keg

Kenworth

Loch Ness
*A lake in Scotland*

Logger

Lumber

Mack

Magnum

Mammoth

Massive

Monster

Moose

Mountain

Mule

Nessie
*A Scottish "monster"
said to live in Loch
Ness*

Pig

Portly

Rhino

Steamboat

Steamer

Stout

Texas

Titan

Tons

Toro
*Spanish for bull*

Triton

Tuba

Tugboat

WalrusOink

Whale

Whopper

# Chapter Five

# Petite Names

Think small. These little names are designed for tiny creatures. Or think fun and attach one of these micro names to your monster pet. Confuse everyone!

| | |
|---|---|
| Acorn | Dinky |
| Agate | Doll |
| *Quartz with colored stripes* | Elf |
| Aphid | Fancy |
| Apple | Fig |
| Atom | Fiji |
| Bean | Flea |
| Berry | Flower |
| Bird | Frog |
| Blossom | Fuzzy |
| Bubble | Gumdrop |
| Bugger | Imp |
| Button | Jellybean |
| Chipmunk | Junior |
| Chiquita | Kermit |
| Clover | Marble |
| Cookie | Micro |
| Cricket | Microbe |
| Daisy | Midget |
| Dinghy | Minnow |
| *A small rowboat or tender* | Missy |

Mittens

Mouse

Muffie

Nipper

Olive

Onion

Peanut

Pebbles

Pewee

Pica

Pigmy

Poco
  *Spanish for "small"*

Puff

Puppet

Quark

Raison

Robin

Sardine

Shorty

Shrimp

Slim

Smidgen

Snowball

Snowflake

Spoon

Squirt

Sweet Pea

Teabag

Teacup

Teaspoon

Thimble

Tiny

Trinket

Turnip

Turtle

Twerp

Whisker

"Now what?"

# Chapter Six

# Aggressive Names

*Aggressive.* Watch out! We're talking TOUGH here: Tough as in nail-spittin', bronco-bustin', macho, Rambo tough. Where do these guys sleep? Anywhere they want. So pick one of these names at your own peril! It may be more than the "foot of the bed" that this creature claims.

| | |
|---|---|
| Ally | Blazer |
| Ambush | Bobcat |
| Amok | Bounty |
| Anarch | Bowie |
| Anvil | *American pioneer knife* |
| Archer | Bowman |
| Armor | Boxer |
| Army | Brazen |
| Arrow | Bruiser |
| Assalt | Buck |
| Ax | Buckshot |
| Badger | Bullet |
| Bandit | Bully |
| Banshee | Cadet |
| Battle | Cannon |
| Bazooka | Casey |
| Bear | Cassius |
| Beast | Catcher |
| Bengal | Chainsaw |
| Blackbelt | Champ |
| Blaze | Charger |

Cheetah

Churchill

Cobra

Colt

Cop

Cossack
*A Slavic cavalryman*

Cyclone

Dagger

Dauntless

Demon

Dingo

Dragon

Eager

Eagle

Fearless

Fighter

Flame

Freeway

Frigate
*A fast warship*

Fullback

Gaff

Gator

Goalie

Grizzly

Guard

Gunner

Hades

Hammer

Harpoon

Hazard

Hero

Hot Dog

Hunter

Jaguar

Jaws

Killer

Knuckles

Lancer
*A mounted, armed soldier*

Leader

Lightning

Lion

Mai-Tai
*A strong rum drink*

Mauser
*A high-powered rifle*

Meatball

Navy

Padlock

Panther

Patton

Pistol

Poison

Python

Rambo

Ranger

Renagade

Revenge

Reward

Rifle

Rocket

Rocky

Rogue

Rommel

Runner

Saber

Sapper
*Bomb squad member*

Scrapper

Searcher

Shark

Shotgun

Slamdunk

Soccer

Soldier

Spear

Spike

Spunky

Stealth
*Secret or sly*

Sting

Storm

Strike

Sturdy

Swagger

SWAT

T-Bone

Tackle

Tarzan

Temper

Thunder

Tiger

Torch

Torque

Tracer

Trapper

Trigger

Triumph

Trojan
*Courageous*

Trooper

Trouble

Turbo

Tyrant

Tyro

Victor

Victoria

*"If I catch the joker who built this doghouse......."*

| | |
|---|---|
| Victory | Wildfire |
| Viking | Wolf |
| Volley | Workout |
| Warden | Yoeman |
| Warrier | Zeppelin |

"He's our dishwasher."

# Chapter Seven

# This 'N That Names

If you are still looking for that pet name that is "just right," it's probably lurking in this chapter. A wide variety of "given names" with a nice ring and rhythm as well as geographical locations (cities, states, countries) are suggested in this section. One might remind you of a place or a name that's just the one!

| | |
|---|---|
| Abe | Babs |
| Abel | Baja |
| Adam | Balboa |
| Aero | Baltic |
| Afro | Bamboo |
| Aggie | **Bangkok** |
| Ajax | *The capital of Thailand* |
| Alfie | Banker |
| Ali | Barnaby |
| Alpine | Barney |
| Alps | Batter |
| Amber | Beacon |
| Anza | Beaver |
| Apache | **Belfast** |
| April | *The capital of Northern Ireland* |
| Artic | Belle |
| Asia | Ben |
| Aspen | **Berkeley** |
| Avis | *A city in California* |
| Aztec | **Berkshire** |
| B.J. | *A city in England* |

Berlin
*A city in Germany*

Beulah

Birdie

Blackie

Blanco/Blanca
*Spanish for white*

Blue

Boston
*Capital of Massachusetts*

Bramble

Brazil

Brindle

Brit

Buffer

Burt

Butch

Cain
*The first son of Adam (biblical)*

Caleb
*Hebrew for "bold"*

Canter

Carlos

Carmel
*A city in California*

Cascade

Chaps

Charley

Checkers

Chesire

Chester

Cheyenne

Chico

Chinook
*Indian tribe*

Chip

Cleo

Cloud

Coco

Codie

Cody

Comet

Concha

Concord

Congo

Corporal

Creole
*Louisiana decendants
of French and Spanish
origin*

Crissy

Crosby

Crystal

Cuba

Custard

Cyprus

Dagmar
*Nordic for "glory of
the day"*

Dakota

Dane

del Mar
*Spanish for "by the
sea"*

Delilah

Denmark

Dennis

Detroit

Dillan

Dinah

Dobie

Doc

Dolly

Dory

Dublin

Dudlee

Duffy

Duncan

Dunlop

Durham
*English short horned
cattle*

Dustin

Dusty

Dutch

East

Eric

Ernie

Eve

Farley

Fitz

Flake

| | |
|---|---|
| Fox | George |
| Foxfire | Goldie |
| Frauline<br>*German for "Miss."* | Gordo |
| | Grammy |
| Frieda | Gucci |
| Fritz | Hannah<br>*Hebrew for Grace* |
| Gambit<br>*A move to gain<br>advantage* | Hans |
| Gato<br>*Spanish for "cat"* | Hardy |

"He's a 'one man' dog, but I'm not the man."

Harper
*A harp player*

Hector
*Greek for "holding fast"*

Heidi

Heinrich

Hogan

Holly

Hormone

Hugo

Hummel

Igo
*A California town near Ono*

Ivan

Jenny

Jet

José

Judah

Jumper

Keeper

Keesha

Kenya
*A nation in Africa*

Kingston

Klamath

Klondike
*A region of the Northwest Territory, Canada*

Lad

Laddie

Laguna

Lassen
*A volcanic mountain in Northern California*

Lassy

League

Lefty

Leib
*German for "love"*

Leif

Leo

Loner

Lonesome

Lucky

Luke

Luna
    *Roman goddess of the moon*

Mabel

Mac

Mackie

Madrid
    *Capital of Spain*

Maggie

Magic

Mark

Marmaduke

Mars

Martha

Marti

Matt

Maui
    *One of the Hawaiian Islands*

Maverick

May

McGee

Medford
    *A city in Oregon*

Memphis
    *A city in Tennessee*

Ming

Mitch

Molly

Monique
    *French for "Monica"*

Montana

Moody

Morris

Mort

Mr. Magoo

Murdock

Murphy

Napa
    *A city in California*

Naples
    *A city in Italy*

Nassau
    *A city in the Bahamas*

Newport

Nibbles

Nicky

Nicole

Noah

North

Norway

Omar
*Hebrew for "eloquent"*

Ono
*A California town
near Igo*

Oscar

Otto

Ozark

Pablo

Paris

Peaches

Pedro
*Spanish for "Peter"*

Penny

Pepe

Peppy

Perro
*Spanish for "dog"*

Perry

Phydough

Piper

Polly

Prancer

Pug

Rambler

Red

Reno
*A city in Nevada*

Ringo

Rojo
*Spanish for "red"*

Roscoe

Rover

Ruffles

Sage

Sally

Sam

Samson
*Biblical man of
enormous strength*

Sancho

Sandy

Sapphire

Sarah

Scarlet

Scottie

Scout

Sean

Sergeant

Shannon

Shasta
*A mountain, lake,
town, and county in
California*

Sheba
*Biblical queen*

Shelby

Shocker

Sid

Sierra
*Mountains; Spanish
for "sawtooth"*

Simon

Sissy

Skip

Sleepy

Smitty

Smokey

Sneezy

Snow

Snowy

Sol
*Spanish for "sun"*

Solo

Sounder

South

Sparkles

Speckles

Star

Stardust

Starlet

Stormy

Stripes

Sullivan

Sundance

Sunday

Sunspot

Sushi
*Japanese fish and rice dish*

Swanee

Sydney

Tabby

Tahoe

Tally

Tampa
*A city in Florida*

Tara

Taurus
*Northern Constellation; second sign of the zodiac*

Thomas

Thumper

Tiber

Tina

Toby

Todd

Tom

Tonga
*South Pacific island country*

Topaz

Topper

Toto

Tracy

Tripper

Trucker

Trusty

Tubby

Tuffy

Tugger

Tulsa
  *A city in Oklahoma*

Tundra

Turk

Tyler

Ulysses

Urban

Utah

Val

Vic

Vinny

Vito

Vladimir

Waldo

Walker

Wanda

West

Wicket

Willie

Willow

Win

Yank

Yellow

Yonkers

York

Yves

Zachary

Zeke

Zeus
  *Greek ruler of the gods*

# Ranking Your Favorite Pet Names

Family or friends can't agree on a final choice? Introduce your pet to the joys (and pitfalls) of democracy. Put it to a vote!

|   | NAME | FOR |
|---|------|-----|
| 1. | _____ | _____ |
| 2. | _____ | _____ |
| 3. | _____ | _____ |
| 4. | _____ | _____ |
| 5. | _____ | _____ |

And the winner is...

_____

# Name Registration With The American Kennel Club

If you wish to register your dog's name with the American Kennel Club (AKC), you should be aware of a few guidelines:

- The name can not be changed once it is registered with the AKC

- AKC allows 37 dogs of each breed to be registered with the same name and may assign a Roman numeral

- Longer and more unique names are more likely to be accepted (you may add your surname to the dog's name to increase the odds of acceptance, e.g. "Brown's Bingo")

- Do not submit names of prominent individuals living or recently deceased, obscene words or Arabic or Roman numerals

For an AKC application or additional information, the address is:

American Kennel Club
51 Madison Avenue
New York, NY 10010

## Chapter Eight

# Bringing Home Your Pet

If you start with a great name for your pet and an appreciation of the animal's basic needs, a sound friendship is likely to follow.

Detailed writings about almost all aspects of pet care and pet behavior are available in dozens of books at your local library, bookstore or pet store. Our purpose in this brief chapter is to point out only a few basic factors to consider in making your pet comfortable in your home — and you comfortable with a new guest: a soon-to-be family member.

There are specific responsibilities for the pet owner and lessons to be learned by the pet, if a sound relationship is to be established. Whether your new friend is a canine or feline, fish or fowl, rabbit or rhino, it has some basic needs, as do all of God's creatures. Most of our suggestions apply mainly to dogs and cats. Other pets that swim or fly or creep or crawl may have their own special needs.

**YOUR PET'S FIRST FEW NIGHTS** in your home may involve a conflict between the pet's choice of a sleeping place and the place *you* want it to snooze. Since the owner is supposed to have at least a slight advantage in intelligence, compromise must be imposed upon the pet: "You *will* sleep in the box at the foot of the bed and you *will* be quiet!" may not work. Cunning and borderline trickery may be required. Some experts suggest placing a hot water bottle wrapped in an old sweater in the pet's bed. Others say a ticking clock will bring peace to the first few nights. Most agree that patience and understanding will soothe all but the most savage beast.

**HOUSE TRAINING YOUR PET** is never going to be at the top of your list of fond memories. But unless your pets are fish, caged, or previously trained, housebreaking is a required learning experience. Again, the experts have written volumes on the subject. Almost every neighborhood has a self-appointed authority. We won't add to the mess (pardon the pun). Our advice is to pick a plan that seems to work with your particular pet. Stay with it. Be patient. *No violence allowed.*

**GOOD FOOD AND EXERCISE** are as important to

the pet as they are to the human machine. Whether your creature is hyperactive or a couch potato will dictate the fuel (food) requirements. Incidentally, a good idea when you first bring home the new pet: continue with the food it is accustomed to, at least for a few days. This will help it feel more "at home" and perhaps keep the stomach calm.

After consulting with a veterinarian and carefully analyzing the mountain of information available on pet nutrition and feeding, you may want to add to or subtract from the pet's diet. Generally, the major pet food manufacturers base their feeding recommendations on the type of pet, its size and its age. Again, you should consider your pet's level of activity.

Pet foods are much more economical when purchased in large quantities, but it is probably advisable to buy small amounts until you find a food that is both nutritional and appealing to the animal. A word of caution: if you occasionally treat your creature to left-over dinner treats, it may acquire a taste for these and insist on a daily gourmet selection. Many vets recommend <u>no</u> table scraps and <u>no</u> real bones. Sorry dogs!

*Don't forget the water!* A dependable source of clean, fresh water is absolutely essential for all our four legged friends — birds too!

**THE BEHAVIOR OF YOUR PET** will be a product of the animal's heredity, background, and the training efforts of the owner. The extent of this training is limited only by your ambition and patience and the intelligence of the pet. For any pet there are certain basic rules of behavior that should not be compromised. The animal will feel more secure in a home with clearly defined boundaries of behavior. For instance, basic obedience for a dog would include compliance with the commands "come," "sit," "heel," "stay" and "down." Easier said than done, but still important — often life or death important.

The numerous approaches to pet training seem to fall into two general categories: positive conditioning and negative conditioning. Without getting into the many subtle technicalities of training, it might be helpful to point out at least some of the highlights.

The main purpose of positive or negative conditioning is to impress upon the animal the unquestioned dominance of the pet owner. This is not to suggest any type of cruelty, but a realistic acceptance of the nature of animal behavior. *You* are the *trainer*. The *pet* is the *trainee*. Don't let this get turned around.

Most pet owners will find the positive approach to training more to their liking. Positive rewards are given for proper behavior, whether it is heeling or tight-rope walking. This can involve lavish verbal praise, petting, or a tasty snack. **Caution:** the snack thing can get out of hand quiet easily. The positive approach can work quiet well with most pets, but can create "spoiled brats" if not tempered with common sense.

Negative conditioning is quite different but need not include visions of short-tempered trainers hanging stubborn dogs with choke chains. *Cruelty has no place in animal training* (or in a decent world, for that matter). Some pets will convince you they have a head of stone and will respond only to the whack of a newspaper on the rear (tempting, but never a good idea, to whack them "long side the head"). Severe negative training might include shaking a dog by the collar to emphasize a point (make sure the animal understands what the "point" is).

At the other extreme, but still "negative," is scolding the pet or just withholding praise. Usually it turns out that once the owner and the pet get smart, scolding is the only negative training ever needed. Praise is much more than just positive. It is longer-lasting and usually better for all concerned.

Whatever your approach to pet training, make sure it is logical, timely, fair and consistent. The world is crazy enough as it is.

**THE HEALTH OF THE PET** is another responsibility that falls on the shoulders of the owner. True, your creature can help by refraining from eating rusty nails and chasing freight trains, but most of the health care (especially preventative) is up to you and the veterinarian.

In fact, a visit to your local vet's office should be one of the first "outings" for you and your pet. The first visit will probably include at least a brief physical check-up, diet and grooming recommendations, and the first of a series of immunizations against the diseases that threaten all pets. Be prepared to part with a significant number of dollars (it might be a good idea to call several offices first, to compare prices). Many vets sponsor more economical "clinics" for such things as rabies vaccinations, spaying and neutering.

You can keep the number of trips to the vet to a minimum by helping your pet avoid some of the nastier parts of this world. For any animal, a clean, safe environment is a good start. For dogs, this means a yard or kennel free of as many hazards as possible. Young dogs seem to have an especially creative ability to get into trouble. They will often chew or eat anything that will stand still, and some that won't. So keep the pet's area free of litter, sharp objects, foxtails and other prickly plants. Avoid fences that could trap your pet or not adequately confine him, as he grows in size and determination (to be on the other side of the fence).

Protection from the elements is critical. Since the domestic animal does not have the freedom to roam and escape the threats of hot and cold weather, the pet owner must anticipate the pet's needs. Your location and the extremes of weather determine the level of protection required.

One major threat to your pet's health that is often overlooked is the four wheel variety. Most pets, especially young ones, have absolutely no sense about the dangers of automobiles and must be restrained and/or watched constantly near any roads.

Even the inside of a car can be hazardous, especially on a hot day. The interior of a parked car can reach lethal temperatures in a matter of minutes. Leave the pet at home or plan to find a shady parking place, and leave the windows open part way.

If your pet becomes sick, any of the following symptoms may be present: high temperature, vomiting, diarrhea, loss of appetite, running eyes and nose, coughing, and lethargy. Professional care should be sought.

The following information should be available to those in charge of caring for your pet(s):

Veterinarian:

Name _____

Address _____

_____

Phone _____

Emergency Phone _____

Medication needed _____

_____

Police Department _____

Fire Department _____

Poison Control _____

Friend or Neighbor _____

Other Information _____

_____

_____

_____

We hope you have found this book
helpful. If you would like to order
additional copies, please send $3.95,
plus $1.05 shipping and handling (CA
residents add appropriate sales tax) to:

Mountain Products
611 Willow Creek Drive
Folsom, CA 95630

Name _____

Address _____

City _____

State _____ Zip _____